A Handy Guide to
Swimming with the Fishes

Stand out from the rest of the school!

Written and Illustrated by
Jess W. MacCallum

IN ARDUA TENDIT

PRESS

SWIMMING WITH THE FISHES
published by In Ardua Tendit Press

© 2003 Jess W. MacCallum

ISBN 0-9749673-0-0

Information available from
In Ardua Tendit Press
464 Leton Drive
Columbia, SC 29210

Printed in the United States of America by Professional Printers, West Columbia, SC [www.ProPrinters.com]

A Brief Introduction...

Originally I was going to come up with some very clever point for this book...all about labeling ourselves and relying too much on the trappings of pop Christian culture for our identity – I thought it might help if any of my Christian brethren took offense to some of the cartoons.

Then I thought I should just be honest. I wrote this book because I thought it was *funny*. As for challenging or enlightening anyone, I can always hope. Probably, most people will be able to laugh at themselves if they see anything familiar. For those upset, sorry.

Jess

really, really, really, really good christian

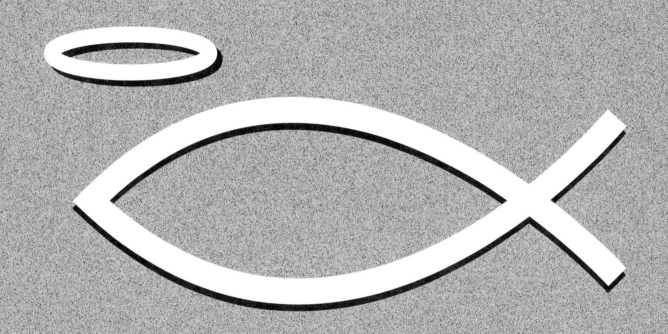

backslider

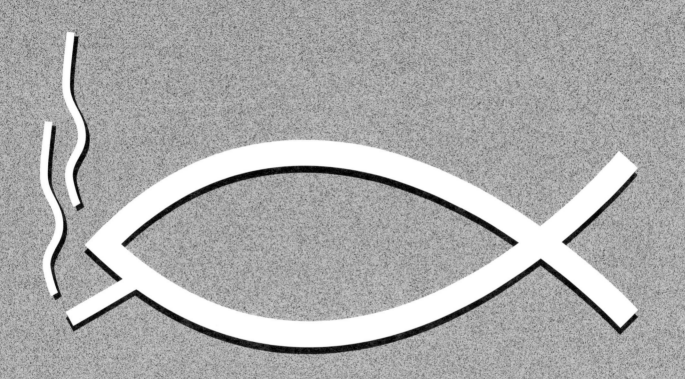

7

hypocrite

preacher's kid

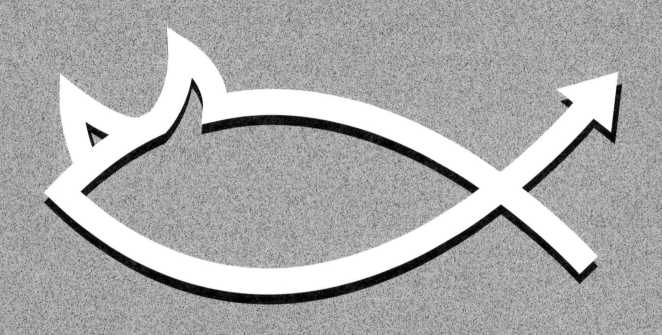

loner

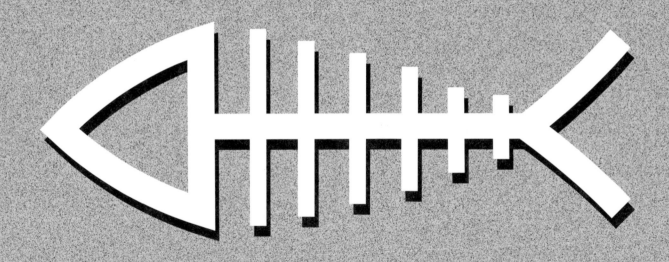

13

early service only

legalist

seminary dropout

19

liberal theologian

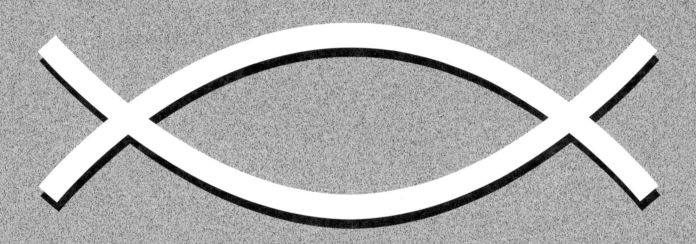

fundamentalist

messianic jew

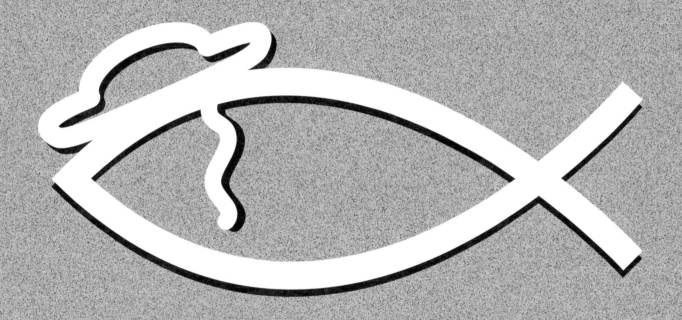

charismatic

27

episcopalian

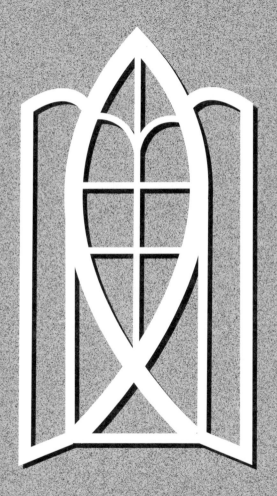

29

presbyterian

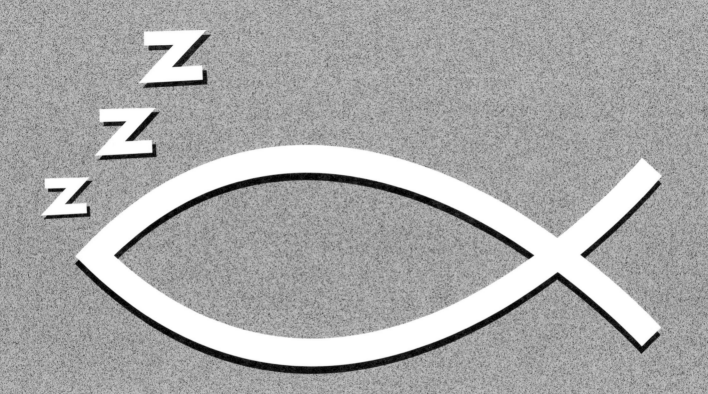

31

southern baptist

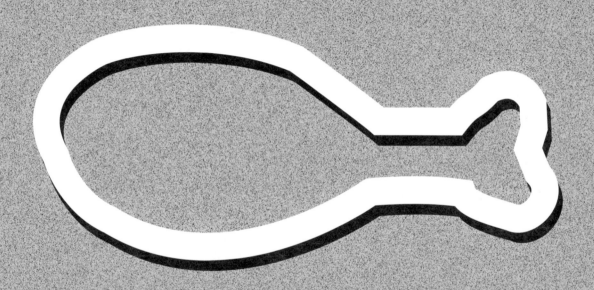

33

5-point calvinist

catholic

televangelist

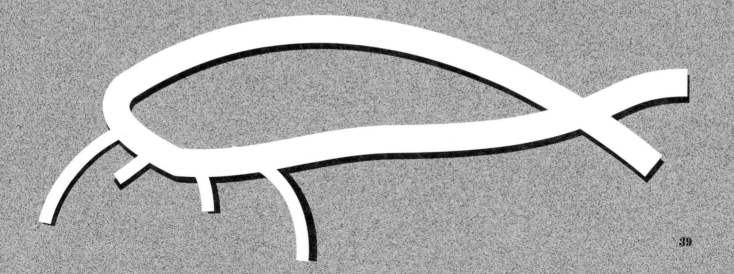

39

late for church

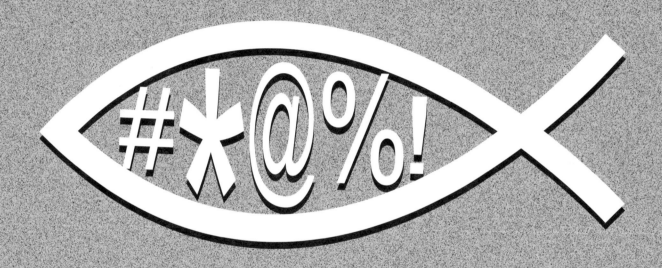

brand new believer

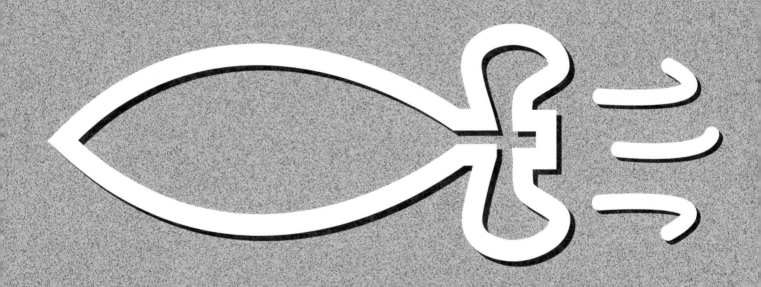

agnostic underneath it all

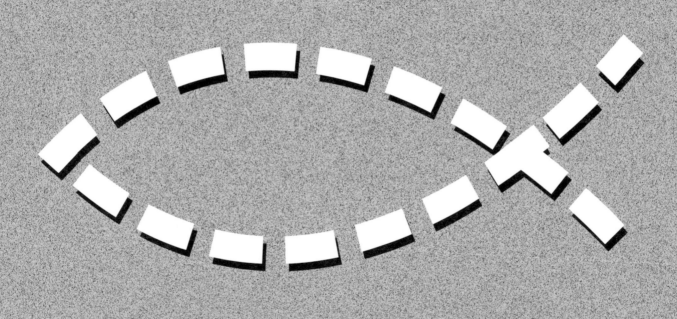

navy chaplain

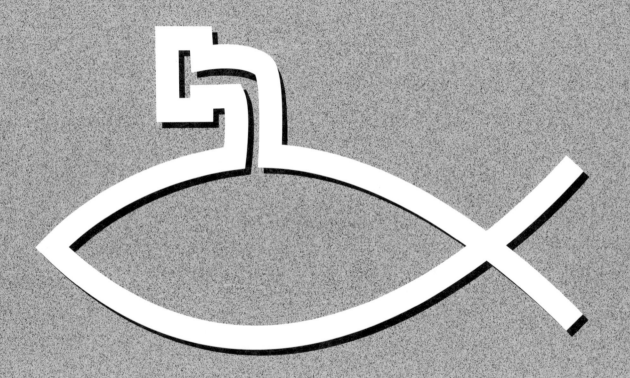

pastor

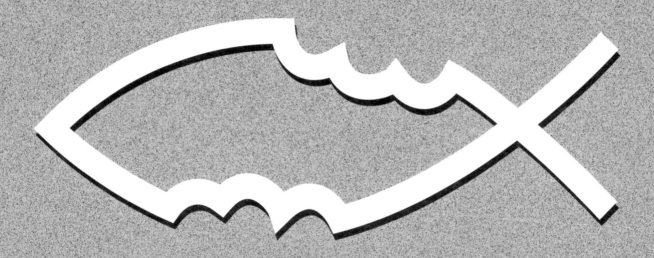

ex-pastor

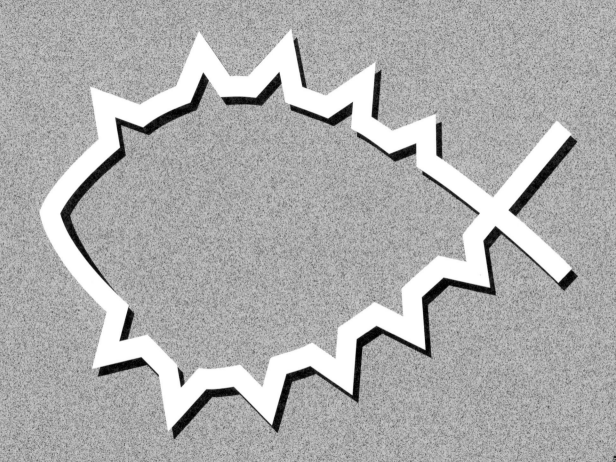

51

deacon

sunday school teacher

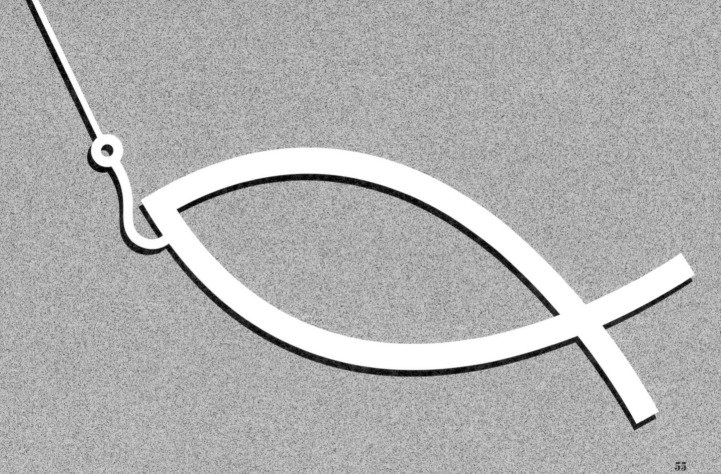

missionary

nursery worker

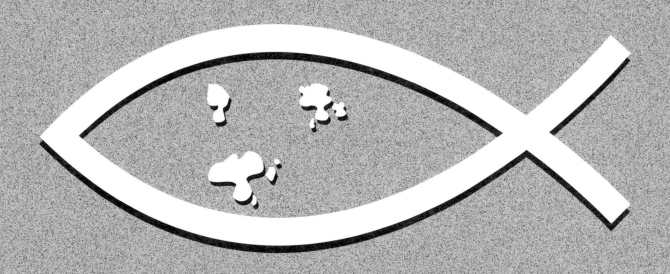

junior high youth leader

church secretary

I have become foolish; you yourselves compelled me.

2 Corinthians 12:11a